To save a Mayd St. George the dragon slew,
A pretty tale if all is told be true.
Most say there are no dragons, and tis sayd
There was no George; pray God there was a mayd.

This US edition © Wooden Books Ltd 2025
Published by Wooden Books LLC,
San Rafael, California

First published in the UK in 2006
by Wooden Books Ltd, Glastonbury, UK

Library of Congress Cataloging-in-Publication Data
Hargreaves, J.
A Little Histroy of Dragons

Library of Congress Cataloging-in-Publication
Data has been applied for

ISBN-10: 1-952178-46-0
ISBN-13: 978-1-952178-46-7

All rights reserved
For permission to reproduce any part of this
firey little book please contact the publishers

Designed and typeset in Glastonbury, UK

Printed in India on FSC® certified papers by
Quarterfold Printabilities Pvt. Ltd.

A LITTLE HISTORY OF DRAGONS

Joyce Hargreaves

"His horns resemble those of a stag, his head that of a camel, his eyes those of a demon, his neck that of a snake, his belly that of a clam, his scales those of a carp, his claws those of an eagle, his soles those of a tiger and his ears those of a cow."

Wang Fu, Han dynasty, describing the nine features of the Lung Dragon

Contents

Introduction	1
What is a Dragon?	2
Tiamat	4
Yggdrasil's Dragons	6
The Sign of the Goddess	8
The Naga	10
Chinese and Japanese Dragons	12
Feng Shui	14
Dragons of the Americas	16
The Hydra	18
The Constellation Draco	20
The Firedrake	22
Typhon	24
The Draconiopides	26
The Worm	28
The Wyvern	30
La Wouivre	32
The Basilisk	34
The Amphisbaena	36
Holy Dragon-Slayers	38
Heraldic and War Dragons	40
Dragons in Alchemy	42
The Serpent Power	44
Dragon Lines	46
The Rainbow Serpent	48
Monsters of Another Age	50
The Earth Dragon	52
Gazetteer of Interesting Dragon Sites	54
Appendix of Chinese Dragons	58

ABOVE: *Winged Sea Dragon.* Plate entitled 'The Creation of Fish and Birds,' by Gustave Doré. Engraving from the illustrated edition of Paradise Lost, 1868.

INTRODUCTION

THE DRAGON is the most nebulous, complex and ambivalent of all the animals that inhabit the jungle of the imagination. This fabulous creature has been the subject of myth and traveller's tales for the last 4,000 years and, although it has never been seen apart from its snake incarnations, its image has been used in religion, alchemy, heraldry and medicine (to name but a few of its aspects), throughout all cultures and histories of the world, primitive, classical, medieval and oriental.

A dragon can primarily be considered to be a symbol of the many different aspects of the powers of the earth, both good and bad. When associated with water, it may represent the fertility of the soil, or herald floods and drought. It can also be seen as a sign of the heat within the earth—appearing in mythology as Typhon, the son of mother Earth, the fire-breathing dragon representing the volcano.

Today sites of dragon legends, hills, caves, mounds and lakes can often be linked to pre-Christian religions, and depictions of the dragon appear in places where they are least expected, like Christian churches.

A pagan dragon can be found in a number of churches with foliage sprouting from its mouth, denoting fertility. Perhaps too the dragon-slayer is equally pagan in concept, and descends from the Green Man and other fertility deities, pressuring the dragon via the spear into releasing its generative forces of nature.

This little book will probably not answer all your questions about dragons, but will, I hope, introduce you to some of the more amazing ideas that surround them.

What is a Dragon?
a wingless flying serpent

EARLY NATURALISTS believed that the dragon was a real animal—often maps of foreign countries were inscribed with the words "here be dragons", usually on areas of unexplored wilderness, and books like the 17th century *Historie of foure-footed Beastes* by Edward Topsell showed depictions of dragons next to reptiles such as lizards and snakes. Today, with our ability to visit nearly every part of the world, we can be almost certain that the dragon, in the general form that we visualise it, does not physically exist anywhere on Earth.

A modern description of a dragon might be that it has four legs, a long snakelike body with a barbed tail, a fierce wyvern's head, bat's wings, sharp claws and teeth, and emits fire from its mouth. However, in earlier times the dragon and serpent shapes were completely interchangeable.

The words *Drakon* and *Draco* were used throughout the Greek and Roman Empires to describe a large snake, and the word 'Dragon' is derived from both of these names. *Drakon* not only referred to a large snake but also to a flying creature (although, like most Chinese dragons, it mysteriously did not need wings to achieve flight). Classical and earlier texts make little distinction between legless serpents and dragons.

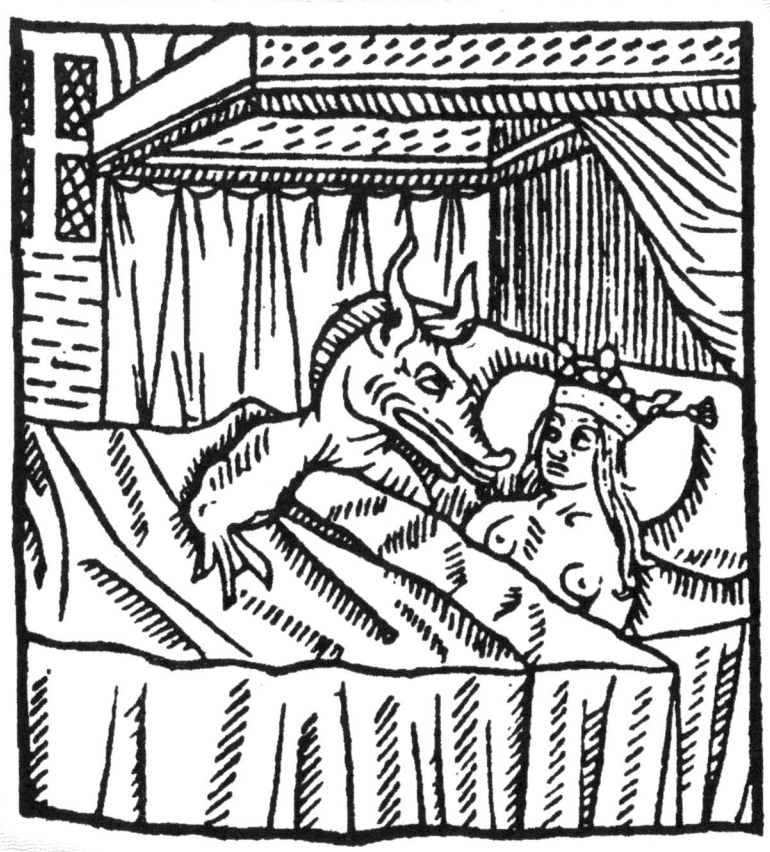

ABOVE: *The dragon's legendary strength and bravery were possibly the reason why Alexander the Great was said to have been fathered by one.*
FACING PAGE: *A winged dragon and serpent from Edward Topsell's 17th century classic treatise* A Historie of Foure-Footed Beastes.

TIAMAT
in the beginning

The account of the creation epic *Enuma Elish* (the Babylonian genesis) was discovered in the form of a long poem on seven tablets excavated at Ninevah in Iraq. The inscriptions date from the 2nd millennium BC, and, when translated, brought the story of the dragoness Tiamat to light.

The tablets tell how in the beginning there was nothing but two elements: *Apsu*, the spirit of fresh water, and *Tiamat*, the spirit of salt water and chaos, portrayed as a dragoness with a serpentine body, horns, and a long tail. In the myth Tiamat gives birth to many children, the Gods, who kill their father to prevent him from destroying them. Their mother's rage at this act leads her to make war against her brood and she spawns eleven monsters; the viper, shark, scorpion man, storm demon, great lion, dragon, mad dog and four nameless ones.

The God Marduk then agrees to fight Tiamat. Armed with a bow and arrows, lightning and a net of four winds, he advances upon his enemy, and after an epic struggle manages to catch Tiamat in his net and drive an evil wind into her mouth, rendering her powerless and destroying her life. He divides Tiamat's body into two parts which become the upper and lower firmaments (the earth and sky)—the Babylonian world order.

Tiamat thus symbolizes primeval chaos, water and darkness.

ABOVE: UPPER: *The imperfect fusion of the traditions of Babylonian and Egyptian mythology created Tiamat, seen here fighting Marduk (drawing based on a design from the second millennium BC).* LOWER, above: *Head of Tiamat, and scorpion man from a Babylonian boundary stone.* FACING PAGE: *Marduk and Dragon.*

YGGDRASIL'S DRAGONS
at the root of the world tree

In Old Norse tradition, the ash tree Yggdrasil, Cosmic Tree of Life, stands at 'the still point of the turning world' supporting the universe. Its branches overhang all the worlds and reach far into the heavens. The three great roots at the base of the tree descend into a tripartite underworld—one twisting towards the frost giants, another reaching the judgement seats of the Aesir, and the third standing over Niflheim where Hel reigns. Underneath Hel's domain dwells the dragon Nidhogg 'The Dread Biter', gnawing at the root from below, attempting to destroy the universe.

While Nidhogg is the evil threatening the universe, the Midgard (or Jornungand) Worm is the bane afflicting the earth, lying in the seas encircling the land with its tail in its mouth, creating and regurgitating the oceans of the world. The legend tells that if its tail is ever wrenched out of its mouth, then calamity will befall the earth.

In the legend the hot-tempered, red-headed, weather-God Thor decides to smite Midgard's worm with his fearsome hammer. He persuades the giant Hymir to take him fishing and, by baiting his strong fishing line with a succulent ox head, succeeds in hooking his prey.

> *"I can tell you this for certain: nobody ever saw a more blood-freezing sight than Thor did, as his eyes goggled down at the serpent and the great worm from below blew a cloud of poison. At that, they say the giant Hymir blenched, then turned yellow in his terror what with the sea swishing into the boat and out of the boat! But Thor grabbed his hammer and flung it above his head just as Hymir fumbled for the knife he used for chopping bait and hacked Thor's fishing rod overboard! The serpent sank down into the depths of the sea".* Snorri Sturluson [1178-1241].

Thor, mortified at his failure, thumps Hymir, upending him into the sea. Later on, Thor and Midgard's Worm eventually kill each other at Ragnarok, the 'Doom of the Gods'.

ABOVE: *The Tree of Life with the Midgard worm circling the Earth. Frontispiece from Northern Antiques, 1847. After Thor's first failed attempt to slay Midguard Worm, the two of them eventually kill each other at Ragnarok, the 'Doom of the Gods'.*

The Sign of the Goddess
coils and cunning curves

From the very earliest times, dragons in the West have been intimately connected with earth goddesses in particular and women in general. In early Mediterranean art, the Mother Goddess is often shown in the company of a serpentine dragon. There is a cylinder seal in existence from the Tigris Euphrates valley, inhabited in 4000 BC by the Sumerians, which shows the great Goddess Bau on the left of the tree of life. Behind her rears a great serpent dragon representing her life giving powers.

In the Pelasgian myth of creation the universal Goddess Eurynome creates the great serpent Ophion to become her mate. Eurynome soon becomes pregnant and gives birth to the 'Universal Egg'. Ophion coils around the egg until it hatches and out falls everything in the Universe from the sun to the smallest ant. But Ophion grows vainglorious and boasts that it is he who is the author of the whole of creation. This enrages Eurynome who hits him over the head with the heel of her shoe, kicks out his teeth and throws him into the dark caves beneath the earth.

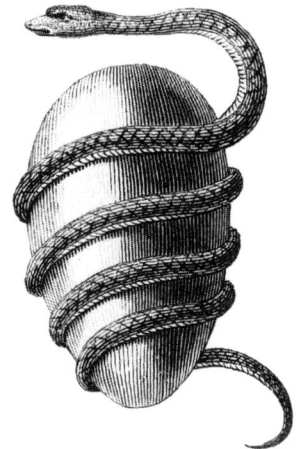

In Egyptian hieroglyphics the term 'goddess' is expressed by the image of a cobra, and the Egyptian Goddess Neith is portrayed as a great golden cobra. Later statuettes of Cretian Goddesses found in the temple of Minos show them holding sacred adders in their hands. Like the Great Goddess these are capable of causing both terror and swift death.

LEFT: Babylonian Boundary Stone 1120BC. ABOVE: Sumerian figure holding two snakes. BELOW: Cretian Goddess holding two adders. FACING PAGE: Ophion coiled around the egg.

THE NAGA
watery serpent spirits

Nagas are the semi-divine, semi-human serpent spirits of Indian origin who are known throughout South East Asia. The Naga King Mucalinda is reputed to have sheltered the meditating Buddha from chilling winds and rain for seven days, protecting him with his hoods and coils. Another legend holds that the king of Ancient Cambodia married a reptilian Naga princess from a huge Pacific kingdom, from whom we are all descended. Nagas and the female Naginis are depicted in three different ways: completely serpentine; human with serpents emerging from the back of the neck; and half human-half serpent.

Their natures are also threefold: animal, human and divine. Dwelling in springs, lakes and rivers, Nagas control all waters, from clouds, rain and fertility to floods and droughts.

Mahayanists divide Nagas into four groups: Divine Nagas who produce clouds and rain; Earthly Nagas whose duty it is to make sure that all outlets are open and that rivers are running freely; Hidden Nagas who guard the treasures of the world; and Heavenly Guardian Nagas who, as 'Guardians of the Threshold' protect the heavenly palace and the temples of many major and minor deities. Guardian Nagas are often portrayed as coiled serpents with human heads, protecting the mysterious sacred pearl of divine wisdom at the center of their labyrinthine coils.

ABOVE LEFT: *A Nagini stone relief from Gondwana, India showing a happy Naga couple with entwined tails c 1100 AD.* ABOVE RIGHT: *Fu-Hsi, the ruler of the mythical third age of China [2852-2738 BC], and his consort Nu Kua were reputedly both Nagas. They are portrayed with their tails entwined in a fourfold pattern. Fu-Hsi holds a compass and Nu Kua a plumb line and a set square - measuring implements to create order out of chaos.* FACING PAGE *Garuda, Vishnu's mount, eloping with enemy Naga Kanya.*

CHINESE & JAPANESE DRAGONS
important invisible families

Ancient Chinese writers describe four types of dragon: the Tian-Lung (Celestial Dragon), who guards the dwellings of the gods; the Fucang-Lung (Dragon of Hidden Treasures), who guards the hidden wealth of the earth; the popular Shen-Lung (Spiritual Dragon) who controls the rain and winds and whose five-toed Imperial image the Emperor alone was permitted to wear; and the celebrated Ti-Lung (Earth Dragon) who holds the rivers and streams in its power.

In all there are nine major types of Chinese dragon, including the Ying-Lung (Winged Dragon), Jiao-Lung (Horned Dragon), Pan-Lung (Coiling Dragon), Huang-Lung (Yellow Dragon) and various others (*see appendix, page 58*). In addition there are nine Dragon Children which adorn many Chinese structures (*see page 58*). The number nine is considered especially lucky in China. Dragons have nine attributes and 117 scales, 81 of them male ($3^2 \times 3^2$) and 36 female ($3^2 \times 2^2$). Chinese dragons are all associated with the masculine Yang force (the phoenix symbolizes Yin).

Chinese and Korean Imperial dragons have five toes on each foot, all other dragons have four toes, but Indonesian and Japanese dragons have three, possibly after the earlier Chinese three-clawed Han style.

Japanese dragons include the Ryu which is a large dragon with no wings, and the Tatsu native Japanese dragon which is smaller but has large wings. In Japanese art the dragon is never wholly visible, instead appearing partially hidden in the swirling winds or waves it represents.

FACING PAGE: *Jade dragon ornament; a dragon carp; the only winged Chinese dragon is the Proper Conduct Dragon; and a dragon pot decoration.* THIS PAGE: *i. Tatsu; ii. Hai Ryio, Japanese bird dragon; iii. Shen Lung; iv. The dragon king, Lung Wang.*

FENG SHUI
and the azure dragon

The 2,500 year-old Chinese art of Feng Shui, or 'wind and water', is used to select an auspicious site and design for a building, where the earth's 'vital spirit' or 'cosmic breath' (*ch'i* in Chinese) is balanced.

The topography of the landscape, its mountains, waterways and valleys, have all been formed by wind and water; it, in turn, affects the local flow of these powerful forces. Four symbolic animals are used:

A hill resembling a huge Black Turtle should lie to the north, to the south the Red Phoenix suggests open vistas, sunshine and water. In the east the Azure Dragon (shown with the Phoenix below) rules jagged rocks like a huge spine, while the White Tiger in the west prefers low, round smooth rocks. As the Azure Dragon is Yang and male, so too are mountains, large rocks, steep waterfalls and ancient pines. The White Tiger represents Yin, the female principle, ruling low-lying places, valleys and damp spots.

ABOVE: *Feng Shui Dragon* by Chow Hon Lam. *A diviner of Feng Shui will study the raised portions of the land, the veins of the dragon, in relation to the valleys, and note auspicious places where there is a harmonious balance of Yin and Yang. The ideal site, or Dragon's Head, is best found beside a hill which rises to the east, northeast or southeast, with one precipitous face and the other sloping gently down to a valley to the south. In general the most favourable position for a structure exists when, looking out over a sparkling stream or slowly meandering river, the hills of the Azure Dragon are positioned to the left and a mountain supports your back.*

DRAGONS OF THE AMERICAS
jewelled watery lightning serpents

The dragons of the North American Indians are more serpentine in shape than many of their European counterparts. They have a snake-like body and are nearly always portrayed with a horn or two, or a jewel, growing out of the tops of their heads. Large and immensely powerful, these serpents are again regarded as water deities and, like Chinese dragons, live mainly in lakes and rivers, creating storms and lightning.

In many North American myths, from Mexico to Alaska, the path of lightning marks the swift darting of lightning snakes, and, also during storms, feathered reptiles (*sisiutl*, *haietlik* or sea wolves) rise out of rivers. These are depicted on masks worn by the Indians for ceremonial dances, symbolizing the fertility associated with rain and lightning.

The feathered serpent also appears widely throughout ancient South America—as the central Aztec deity Quetzalcoatl (literally 'quetzal-bird snake'), known to the Maya as Kukulkan, and in 3000 year-old Olmec representations. As the magical morning star, Venus, Quetzalcoatl emerges from the mouth of the earthbound feathered serpent. The inventor of the calendar, he is also, like the Chinese Yellow Dragon, credited with bringing the art of writing to mankind.

Note the wind and water combination of feathers and serpent.

ABOVE: *Wall relief, Pyramid of the Feathered Serpent, Xochicalco, Mexico, c 800AD.* BELOW: *Quetzalcoatl as the Feathered Serpent, Tenochtitlan, Mexico;* FACING PAGE: *Quetzalcoatl from a manuscript; Haietlik Serpent; Canadian 442 Squadron Haietlik Lightning Snake motif.*

THE HYDRA
many-headed water dragon

The mythological Hydra embodies the fertilizing powers of water. Today, any living thing that is hard to destroy may be called 'hydra-headed'. One of the earliest representations of the Hydra appears on a 1400 BC cylinder seal from Syria, and portrays part of a myth where the fertility god Baal conquers the seven-headed dragon Latan, a creature identified with the watery forces of chaos and disorder.

In Greek mythology, the description of Heracles' fight with the Lernaean Hydra shows her powers of renewal (*see two illustrations, opposite*). The Hydra was an awe-inspiring sight—she had a prodigious dog-like body and eight or nine reptilian heads (one of which was immortal). For every head that Heracles cut off, the beast reproduced it twofold until he set the neighbouring woodland alight and with red-hot brands seared the necks, finally burying the immortal head beneath a rock. This battle seems to record the suppression of the Lernaean fertility rites, as new priestesses, like the regenerated heads of the Hydra, constantly appeared in the temple on the banks of the river Anymone until it was burned down.

The Bible has its own famous Hydra in *Revelations* 12:3: *"and behold a great red dragon, having seven heads and ten horns, and seven crowns upon his heads."*

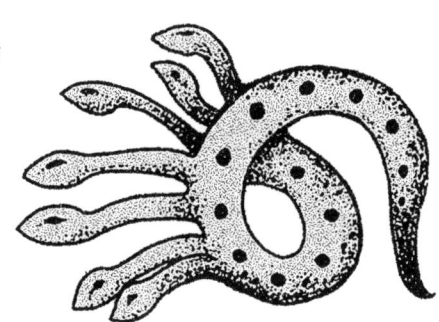

THE CONSTELLATION DRACO
winding around the pole

The Greek word *Drakon* comes from a verb meaning 'to see' or 'to watch' and Dragons have great reputations as guardians of wisdom and treasure. In Greek mythology the dragon Ladon guarded the apples on the Tree of the Hesperides for the Goddess Hera. Ladon, who was the parthenogenous (virgin-born) son of Mother Earth, had 100 heads and, with 200 keen eyes, was the obvious choice for a guardian. However, even with these advantages, he was no match for the hero Heracles who shot him with an arrow and stole the apples. To commemorate this feat Heracles bore the likeness of a Dragon on his shield, described by Homer as: *"A scaly horror of a Dragon, coiled full in the central field, unspeakable, with eyes oblique, retorted, that askant shot gleaming fire."*

The Goddess Hera wept bitterly at the death of Ladon and set his image among the stars as the constellation of the serpent Draco. Draco, also known as the Red Dragon, is a large constellation of stars which winds around the celestial and the ecliptic north poles and can be seen in the northern sky positioned close to Heracles.

Another Greek myth tells a different story—of the time that Zeus and his followers battled with the gods of an earlier mythological order high on Mount Olympus. In the struggle that ensued the new gods drove out the old ones and Draco, who as a Lord of Chaos was counted among the elder gods, was cast into the sky by the Goddess Athene. She sent his body spinning into a knotted circle where he remains to this day, inextricably tangled with the north pole, and daily turning with it on the slowly drifting axis of the northern sky. In fact, the star Thuban (Draconis), third from the tip of Draco's tail, was the pole star, centre of the heavens, in 2700 BC, the age of Stonehenge and ancient Egypt.

ABOVE: Draco, from a 12th century Sufi book of constellations, and a circular representation of some of the circumpolar stars showing Heracles brandishing his club while standing on the head of Draco.

THE FIREDRAKE
shooting across the sky

Heavenly comets, shooting stars (meteors), lightning and the Aurorae Borealis (northern lights) have long caused wonderment on earth, and historically they have all been documented somewhere as dragons. This includes the extraordinary phenomenon called the *draco volans*—the Firedrake—the glittering celestial event noted by early medieval meteorologists. The Anglo-Saxon Chronicle records that *"... excessive whirlwinds, lightning, storms and fiery dragons were seen flying in the sky."*

A brilliant head attached to a long luminous tail gives a comet a very draconian appearance, though some thought that it consisted merely of a conglomeration of vapour in the lower air. In 1571 William Fulke said of it:- *"I suppose it was a flying dragon, wherof we speake, very fearfull to loke upon as though he had life, because he moueth, where as he is nothing els but cloudes and smoke ..."*

The *Oxford English Dictionary* describes the term 'Firedrake' as applying to meteors and, in Scotland, strange lights in the sky were often called Fiery Drakes. In northern mythology, Firedrakes were cave-dwelling dragons who guarded hoards of gold in gravemounds and because of this were believed to be the spirits of the departed. In time they became the symbols of triumph over death. In the Norse Volsunga saga, the giant Fafnir transforms himself into one of these fire dragons and carries his gold into a remote cave where he stays there quite alone. Fafnir's brother Regin persuades a young student, Sigurd, to kill him. The youth is able to do this, and afterwards cooks the dragon's heart but accidentally sucks his finger. As the dragon's blood touches his lips he understands the language of birds, and these, like the dying Fafnir, inform him that Regin will try to kill him. So he finally draws his sword and cuts off Regin's head.

ABOVE: Arthur Rackham's drawing of the dragon Fafnir from 'The Ring of the Nibelung'.

Typhon
the fire dragon

It is not just air and water which flow. Fire too undulates, and the ancestor of all fire-breathing dragons is surely the monstrous Greek god Typhon. The final son of Gaia, the Earth Mother, and fathered by Tartarus, the void, he represents one of her most destructive aspects. His body from the thighs down was composed of coiling, poisonous serpents, his wings blacked out the light of the sun and his heads touched the stars. A most terrifying sight, Hesiod describes him thus:

> *"...and from his shoulders grew a hundred serpent's heads, heads of a dread dragon that licked with dusky tongues, and from the eyes of his wonderous heads fires flashed beneath his brows and from all his heads fire burned as he glared."*

Zeus waged a bitter battle with the monster, eventually driving Typhon to Sicily where he was crushed under the volcano Mount Etna. Today his fires still belch forth from its core and his mouth spews flaming rocks and larva, the fiery molten earth which shapes the world.

Typhon also rules the fourth element, air, in its dangerously hot form. Hot winds coil and spiral to produce the cyclonic storms we still call 'typhoons', the word having been borrowed by the Persians and Arabs.

IMAGO TYPHONIS
IVXTA APOLLODORVM.

Oriens / Occidens

Typhon Omne malum physicum

Typhon Omne malum Ethicum

Interpretatio Ethica iuxta Synesium.

Imago hominis Typhonij.

A Confusio mentis seu intellectus.
B Æstus concupiscentiæ.
C Libido & lingua virulenta.
D Opera mala.
E Leuitas mentis, & iactabunda ostentatio.
G Hypocrisis.
H Inuidiæ rabies per serpentes.
I Ira & furor animi.
K Inconstantia & lubricitas mentis.

Interpretatio Physica iuxta Plutarchum.

A Confusio elementorum in suprema regione aëris.
B Ignearum exhalationum noxia vis.
C Ardor Martius omnia adurens.
D Vis noxia omnes Mundi partes peruadens.
E Celeritas ventorum Typhonicorum.
G Perturbatio aëris per noxias ventorum qualitates.
H Corruptio aëris ex pernitiosis ventorum flatibus.
I Fulminis, tonitruum, & fulguris eius.
K Montibus, & mari maximè dominantur venti.

ABOVE: *Imago Typhonis*, from *Oedipus Aegyptiacus* by Athanasius Kircher, 1652.

THE DRACONIOPIDES
taste the fruit of the tree

When a new religion conquers an earlier one, old customs and gods are either incorporated into the new order or they become demonized. In the Judeo-Christian era the dragon was in for a shock. While Christianity personified the Egyptian Osiris and Greek Dionysus in the figure of Jesus, ancient horned and fertility deities were combined into the sinister horned and hooved figure of Satan, while dragons of wisdom, flow and fertility became envoys of negative, destructive power.

Thus a serpentine dragon, Lilith, appears at the very beginning of the Bible in the Garden of Eden persuading Eve to eat forbidden fruit—a Hebrew text reminds us "... for before Eve was Lilith". She is described elsewhere as the first wife of Adam who refused to lie beneath him (and obey his commands), so when Adam spurned Lilith and married Eve in the garden of Eden, she revenged herself on Adam's wife. She further appears as a night phantom and enemy of newborn babies—the very opposite of a good and loving mother. Lilith is thus probably a distortion of a venerable ancient deity worshipped long before Judaism.

Interestingly, the later Roman depiction of the ancient Egyptian goddess Isis, who ruled fertility and motherhood, was as a snake with a human head. In medieval times Lilith was shown coiled around the Tree of Knowledge, with the head of a beautiful woman and the body of a serpent, tempting Eve with the apple (*opposite*).

LEFT: *The Draconiopides in the Garden of Eden, stained glass window, Ulm Cathedral, Germany, 1420.* BELOW: *Lilith tempting Eve, German woodcut, 1470.* BOTTOM: *Temptation and Expulsion, after Michaelangelo, Sistine Chapel, Rome. In medieval times. A creature with the head of a beautiful woman and the body of a serpent is known as a Draconiopides.* FACING PAGE: *Draconiopedes peering round the Tree of Life at Eve, who offers Adam the forbidden apple.*

The Worm
coiled around a hill

A Northern European dragon who has a serpentine shape but lacks wings or legs is termed a 'Worm' or 'Lindworm', from the Norse *ormr* meaning 'dragon'. The embodiment of stuck or stagnant energies, the Worm has very few redeeming features. Described as a serpent with a horned, reptilian or horse-like head, its traditional natural habitat is in wet or damp places, like lakes, wells, the sea, or bogs, where it may also sometimes be found coiled around a small conical hill.

There are many references to the Worm in Great Britain; the Gurt Vurm of Shervage Wood lived in Somerset, and near Pitempton, in Scotland, is the broken base of a Pictish cross called Martin's Stone. Carved at its base is a fat serpent lying across a zig-zag line. It is here, in legend, that a wormlike dragon was slain by a man named Martin.

The legend of the Northumbrian Lambton Worm tells of the Lambton heir catching an unpleasant-looking worm while fishing, which he throws into a well. There it grows and grows until it is a danger to everything. The heir rectifies his mistake by standing on a stone in the middle of a river wearing a knife-studded suit of armor.

When the worm tries to crush him, its body is cut to pieces which are swept away in the river's fast-flowing current, thus preventing it from regenerating.

Childe Wynd thrice kisses the Laidly Worm & rescues his Sister the Princess Margaret.

TOP LEFT: The Laidly Worm, of Spindlestone Heugh, is a tale of a Northumberland princess, turned into a dragon by a jealous stepmother. OTHER IMAGES on this page show the Lambton Worm, and the hero with the spikey armour.

THE LAMBTON WORM

The Wyvern
beware the eyes

Early depictions of the dragon show it in the form of a serpent, and the Wyvern is halfway between the shape of a Worm and a fully-fledged four-legged dragon. There are Chinese, Toltec and Pictish equivalents of the beast, and possibly these were the models that were used to change the shape of the visually-not-very-dynamic serpentine version.

When illustrating a fight between a courageous hero or saint and a dragon, a serpent can look a little undramatic or not particularly vicious; it needs—in contemporary parlance—a makeover, to appear more aggressive and formidable while doing battle with the valorous hero.

Over a period between the 11th and 12th centuries AD changes were seen in the Worm's serpentine shape in sculpture and manuscript art. It was transformed into a ferocious beast with bat-like wings, a fierce looking head and two legs, and was named a Wyvern, from the French *wivere* meaning 'viper' and 'life', its new name invoking the vital flowing energies of the dragon. But it was also inverted in some European countries and depicted as a vicious and fierce predator, taking instead of giving life. In some cases the Wyvern does not even have to catch its victims for it possesses a strange power over other living things—if a creature looks into a Wyvern's glittering emerald eyes, it will be hypnotized and lured into its greedy mouth.

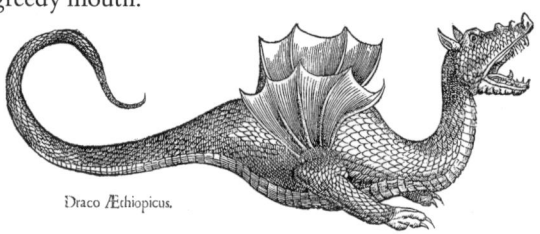

Draco Æthiopicus.

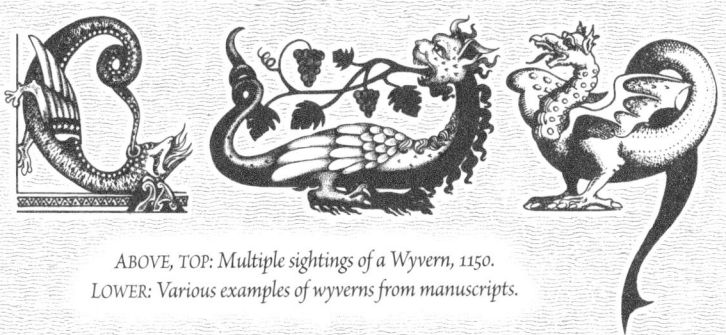

ABOVE, TOP: Multiple sightings of a Wyvern, 1150.
LOWER: Various examples of wyverns from manuscripts.

La Wouivre
a natural mystic flowing through the air

Portrayed with the head and upper body of a voluptuous woman the beneficent French Wyvern known as the Wouivre has a ruby set into her head between her eyes, or in place of them, by which she can guide herself through the underworld. In some traditions this precious eye is a luminous ball that hangs in the air in front of her. The only chance to steal her jewel is when she is bathing and leaves the stone unguarded on the ground. If that should happen she would be as blind as a bat.

In his 1387 *Le Noble Hystoire de Luzignan*, Jean d'Arras tells the ancient story of Melusine or Melusina, the Countess of Lusignan, who was reputed to have been transformed into an immortal Wouivre. Over the ages which followed she watched over her descendants, warning them of impending disasters by screeching three times.

The term *Wouivre* is also given to snakes that glide and to rivers that snake, including the subtle telluric currents of geomancy. As such the Wouivre is also related to the *genius loci*, the 'spirit of the place', as she hovers protectively over the highlands and the countryside. She dwells in mountainous regions, ruins, abandoned chateaux and frequents the area around Nevers, where her name is transformed into 'Wivre'.

ABOVE: *A Medieval woodcut of Melusine of Avalon, Countess of Lusignan, a Wouivre with a blue and white tail. On Saturdays she would hide from her husband and turn into a Dragon. When he found out she retreated to a town in the French Alps, and lived on the Apollo-Athena line (p. 47).*

THE BASILISK
king of serpents

The Basilisk is the king of serpents, and monarch of smaller reptiles. In early pictures it appears as a serpent with a narrow pointed head topped by three crest-like excrescences, but it was later portrayed with a thicker and heavier body, two bird-like legs and a crown instead of a crest.

The Basilisk lives in the desert, which it creates through its venomous withering breath. One searing glance from its glowing eyes is enough to kill a man instantly. This murderous stare can also be the Basilisk's downfall for the sight of its reflected stare in a mirror will strike it dead. Two creatures can kill a Basilisk: the weasel (by biting it to death) and the cockerel (whose crowing sends it into a terminal fit).

During the first century AD the deserts of North Africa were said to be infested with these creatures and desert travellers often used to take a number of cockerels as protection against them. But reports soon began describing a different type of Basilisk which had the head of a cock. This creature was at first called a Basilcock and later a Cockatrice. The Cockatrice was born from a toughened, spherical, unshelled egg laid by a seven-year-old cock under Sirius the dog star and hatched by a toad or snake on a dung heap.

Various images showing Cockatrices (opposite left, above right), and Basilisks (opposite right, above, and right, as portrayed by Athanasius Kircher in the 1600s). To medieval Christians, the cockatrice represented sin and sudden death and was one of the four aspects of the devil.

THE AMPHISBAENA
the double-headed dragon

The Amphisbaena is a double-headed dragon or serpent, usually portrayed with bird's claws, pointed bats wings and the extra head at the end of its tail. It is said to be capable of giving a venomous bite with both sets of fangs. Amphisbaenas are hard to kill: when cut in half, the two parts can join back together, and it can also cover ground very fast, both backwards and forwards (its name in Greek means "goes both ways"). In 1893 John Greenleaf Whittier wrote about it in a poem *The Double-headed Snake of Newbury*.

'For he carried a head where his tail should be,
  And the two of course could never agree,
But wriggled about with main and might,
  Now to the left and now to the right;
Pulling and twisting this way and that,
  Neither knew what the other was at.'

According to Pliny the Elder, the amphisbaena is reputed to give protection in pregnancy when alive and cure rheumatism when dead—a typically ambivalent state of affairs.

The dual nature of this two-headed beast also describes the solar (positive, active, masculine) and lunar (negative, passive, feminine) forces of the earth as symbolized by the caduceus. In Christian symbolism, unsurprisingly, it is the negative side of the amphisbaena which receives emphasis, appearing as the 'Adversary'—a concept later attached to the devil—which must be fought and mastered by heroes and saints. Modern psychology in fact defines a dragon as 'something terrible to overcome', for only he who conquers a dragon becomes a hero.

TOP LEFT: St. Michael fighting an Amphisbaena, detail of a piece of embroidery.

ABOVE: Two examples of Amphisbaenas from medieval and modern artworks.

LEFT: Amphisbaena on gold, from an early illuminated manuscript.

OPPOSITE: Amphisbaena from an early book.

HOLY DRAGON-SLAYERS
fixing the serpent

Pictures of dragon-slayers often show the saint's spear forcing the dragon's head to the earth, or poised in front of its open mouth. This echoes the traditional method of recharging serpentine, telluric currents by piercing the ground with a rod to fix the energy flow.

Earthly St George, patron saint of England, is often identified with earlier pagan gods like the fertility figure of the Green Man or Jack-in-the-Green and especially with the Celtic God Belinus, who also fought with a dragon. Historically, however, he poses a problem as none of his British contenders have any reputed connection with a dragon.

Heavenly St Michael is the chief archangel, and represents the sun. Often invoked for his healing energies, he rules high places and mediates health-giving solar powers, taking over the roles of the Graeco-Roman Aesculapius and the Hellenic Seraphis both of whom have a healing serpent as their symbol. *The Bible* describes St Michael's battle with the dragon:

> *"Michael and his angels fought against the dragon, and the dragon fought and his angels and prevailed not ... he was cast out into the earth."*

ABOVE LEFT: After Raphael, an early 1900's engraving by J. L. Petit. ABOVE RIGHT: Durer's etching of St. Michael casting out the dragon. BELOW: A drawing by F Anstey of the slaying of a family of dragons. OPPOSITE, LEFT TO RIGHT: The three most important Christian dragon-killing saints: St Michael; St Margaret (who, though eaten by a dragon, burst it asunder with her cross); and St George.

Heraldic & War Dragons
red, white and green

The heraldic dragon is one of the most artistic of all heraldic creations and the one with which we are most familiar today. Its four legs, neck and back are covered with scales, while the under part of its body is scaled in rolls of a much larger size. Its tongue and tail are barbed and its wings are those of a bat. Although heraldry is essentially medieval in origin, the use of the dragon as a personal device was in use from much earlier times—Marduk, slayer of Tiamat (*see page 4*), had a dragon as his emblem and Heracles bore a dragon effigy on his shield.

The legend of the Welsh flag describes how King Vortigern designed a fortress at Dinas Emrys which proved impossible to build for as soon as a wall was raised, it collapsed. A lad named Merlin said that beneath the foundations two dragons were battling in an underground lake, shaking the walls and causing them to fall. This proved to be true, for a red dragon and a white dragon were seen there fighting, and the red dragon eventually obtained suzerainty. The legend is based on history, and probably describes an actual battle, as when armies rode out it was the custom for each side to group beneath a dragon standard of an identifying color. In this particular instance the red dragon, the British (or Welsh), overcame the white dragon, the Saxons (or English). A red dragon on a green and white ground, known as the Red Dragon of Cadwallader, later became the national flag of Wales.

Merlin became adviser to King Arthur, son of Uther Pendragon who had a vision of a flaming dragon which was interpreted as a sign that he would become king. Uther took the name 'Pendragon' ('Head Dragon'), and both he and Arthur used the dragon as their heraldic symbols on their arms and helmets.

LEFT: *A dragon war machine from Roberto Valtrio's 'De Re Militari'. Dragons on banners, standards and shields are signs of valour and courage and represent the power of a ruler. The draco windsock banner was widely used in the Roman Empire, and the Persians and Scythians also bore dragons on their standards. A windsock consisted of a pole, held by a soldier called a Dragonarius, which had a carved wooden Dragon's head mounted on top of it. A tube of cloth was attached to the head and, when the banner was held aloft, it filled with wind, writhing and billowing like a living creature. This scared the enemy and assisted the archers by showing them the strength and direction of the wind. Even today there is a regiment of English guards called 'Dragoons'.*

ABOVE: LEFT: *Heraldic drawing showing enlightenment (figure) coming out of wisdom (dragon).* CENTRE: *A German dragon, known as the Lindwurm, of the same kind as the Red Dragon of Wales, from A.C. Fox-Davies's "A Complete Guide to Heraldry".* RIGHT: *Another heraldic dragon.*

DRAGONS IN ALCHEMY
the mysteries of the earth

The literature surrounding the secretive and magical art of Alchemy is rich with dragons, where they assist in the physical and psychological chemistry lessons and appear in different ways for various hidden purposes— "The dragon slays itself, weds itself, impregnates itself."

The most famous of all alchemical dragons is the Ouroboros, the great serpent devouring itself, as depicted romantically on the front of this book, and reminding the student that "All is One" and that the universe undergoes periodic cycles of destruction and creation. Winged dragons in alchemy generally represent the mercurial volatile elements, i.e. substances in the vessel which can evaporate, while wingless dragons signify fixed ones, although many alchemists regard all dragons as representing Mercury, the spirit, or life force. Dragons sometimes fight, where they illustrate psychic disorder or the conflict between unrefined Sulphur (soul) and Mercury (spirit). The two-headed amphisbaena (*page 36*) becomes, in alchemy, the caduceus (*below, left and right*), the winged rod with two serpents twined about it carried by youthful Hermes and symbolizing the harmonious intertwining marriage of opposites which is the alchemist's objective.

In alchemical symbolism, it is only by the killing of the dragon that the transmutation of the Prima Materia can take place and so produce Luna, the White Queen or unicorn, the virgin divinity in nature.

LEFT: Sol and Luna hunting and subduing the dragon. Their fear of the uncontrolled dragon power makes the dragon cower. Later they will no longer fear the dragon but embrace it and learn from it. Emblem 50 from Michael Maier Atlanta Fugiens: De Secretis Naturae Chymica, 1617.

LEFT: A man sleeps in his grave encoiled and embraced by the Universal Soul of the Earth spirit. The soul recognises the labyrinthine ways of dragon and is awakened by it to the connected life. Emblem from Michael Maier Atlanta Fugiens: De Secretis Naturae Chymica, 1617.

THE SERPENT POWER
the kundalini of the earth

The image of the caduceus, with its pair of serpents climbing up a central staff, is very ancient indeed, and finds its most widespread application in the yogic and tantric traditions of ancient India. Here it appears as the essential blueprint for the human body—a pair of serpent heads springing from the base of the spine, volatising (i.e., gaining wings) by spiraling upwards toward the heavens and framing the seven spinning energy centers known as the chakras.

This amphisbaena embodies a power known as *kundalini*, similar to the Chinese *ch'i* and Japanese *qi*, and, like the Chinese *yin* and *yang*, thought of as consisting of a balance of female and male energies. In India these are Shakti, the mother of the universe, and Shiva, the purifier (*shown together below left*). A central purpose of yogic physical and mental exercises is to awaken the kundalini and allow it to rise and transform the individual.

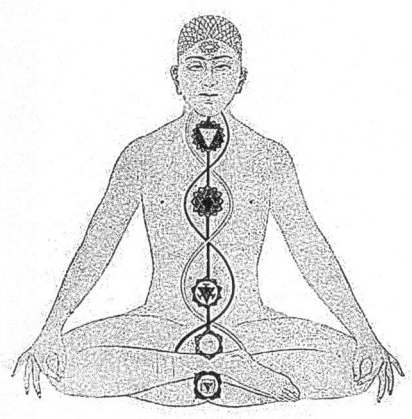

TOP LEFT: *An alchemical emblem showing the divine hermaphrodite fusing with the serpent energies of the awakening kundalini which rises and spirals from a mastered amphisbaena on which the figure stands.*

ABOVE: *The seven chakras or psychic centres of the ancient Indian system, corresponding to the seven endocrine glands of modern biology. These are only truly awakened when the serpent power is liberated.*

LEFT: *According to the tantric yogic tradition Kundalini is curled up in the rear part of the root base chakra in three and a half turns around the sacrum. When awakened the serpent energies rise up the spine as a transformative caduceus of balanced male (Shiva) and female (Shakti) principles allowing the individual to truly fuse with the universe.*

Dragon Lines
the blood runs deep

The term 'ley' or 'ley line' denotes a series of straight alignments of ancient sites such as standing stones, hill forts, sacred springs and ancient churches, many of which have connections with dragon mythology.

The longest of the English leys is the St Michael's line of dragon sites (*shown below*) that stretches along the May Day sunrise line from the westerly tip of Cornwall through St Michael's Mount, Glastonbury, Avebury and Bury St Edmunds. Recently, two huge serpentine energy currents have also been discovered by dowsers following the alignment: one is male and follows the high places, often churches dedicated to St Michael; the other female current stays low and passes through wells, springs and churches dedicated to St Mary and Margaret.

Another long straight alignment traces an alignment of sacred sites across Europe. This too appears to consist of two dowseable currents, one male (Apollo) and one female (Athena) forming a huge landscape caduceus across Europe, marking the passageway of the Earth Spirit.

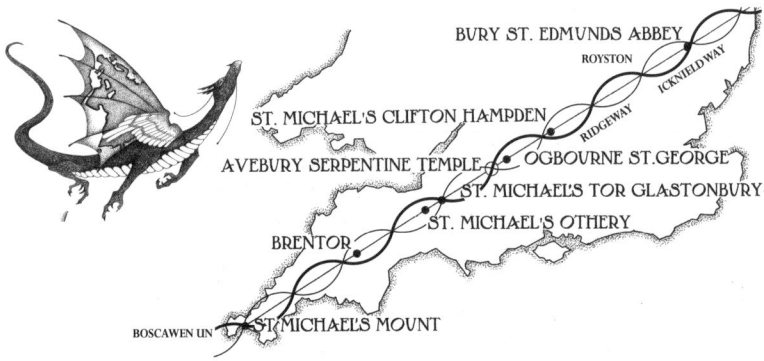

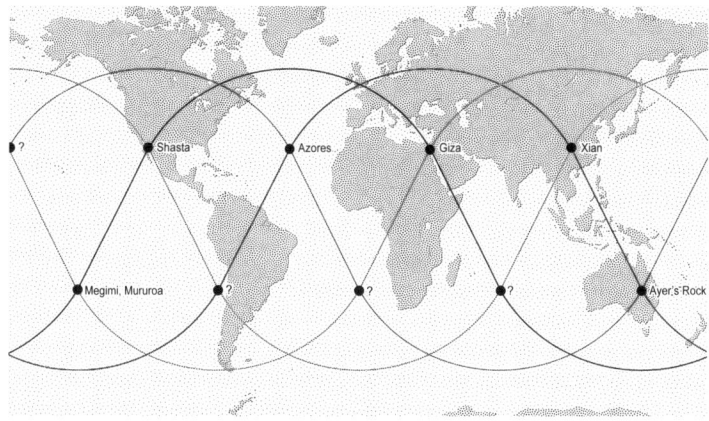

ABOVE: A suggestive plait of three global dragons lines, with ten crossing places. Two further points at the poles give twelve in all, the number of vertices of an icosahedron. FACING PAGE: England's 'Michael Line' joins the easternmost and westernmost tips of England and is supported by a pair of serpentine energy lines which pass through a vast number of ancient sites. BELOW: The Apollo-Athena line, with its similar pair of male and female energy currents (see pages 57 & 231). These start out in Ireland passing through sites dedicated to Michael and Mary respectively, but by the time they reach Greece are passing through temples dedicated to Apollo and Athena.

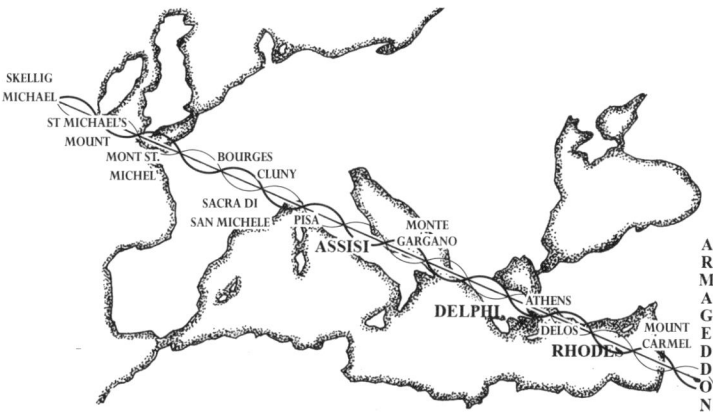

THE RAINBOW SERPENT
always half invisible

The idea of dragon or serpent lines in the landscape finds its earliest expression in the art and myths of the native peoples of Africa and Australia. In western and central Africa a pair of snakes, Danbhalah (the male divine serpent) and Aida Hwedo (the female rainbow serpent) represent wisdom incarnate, and in Australia, as in so many ancient cultures, the earliest legend of all concerns a very similar reptile.

The Aboriginal story begins in the distant Dreamtime when there were no animals, birds, trees, bushes, hills or mountains. The Great Rainbow Serpent stirred and set off to look for his own tribe. In the course of his wanderings he left huge impressions on the landscape, forming gorges, mountains, creeks, rivers and hills, both destroying and creating the environment. When he tired of shaping the earth he dragged his massive body into a water hole and sank into its depths. Today he is long gone, but his spirit still shines after rains fall—as the rainbow.

The 'songlines' or 'dreamings' left by the Rainbow Serpent and other creation beings are still marked by alignments of natural features, some visible and some invisible. They criss-cross the entire continent of Australia, each possessing its own storyline and song structure.

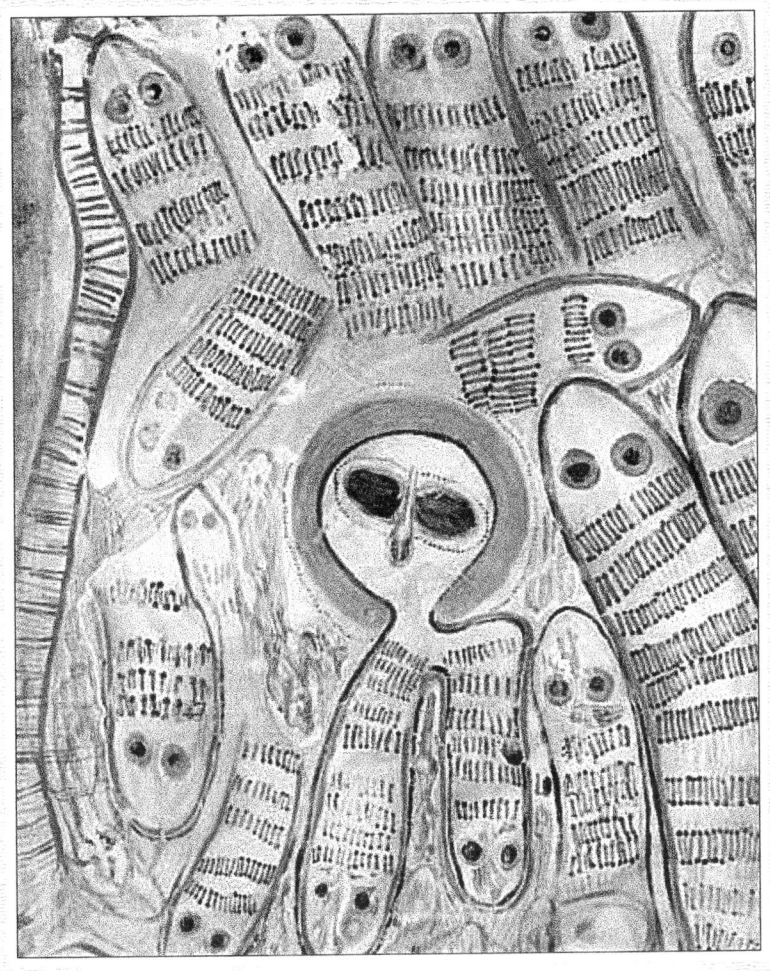

ABOVE: A 50,000 year-old Australian aboriginal rock painting of a human face surrounded by nearly 20 serpent spirit beings.

MONSTERS OF ANOTHER AGE
living dragons and dragon bones

Today we live within the modern myth of science. It tells of a long-gone age where the earth was walked by lizards called dinosaurs. Could dragon legends actually contain dim memories of real animals?

On the Indonesian island of Komodo off Indonesia lives a large four-legged, long tailed lizard known as a Komodo dragon. Any explorer coming across one might easily be forgiven for imagining that they had come across some kind of wyvern (*page 30*). A Komodo dragon is a living dinosaur, but reptiles like snakes and lizards are not the only descendants of dinosaurs—far more common in fact are all birds.

On the island of New Zealand a giant flightless bird known as the Moa (*below left*) lived until only a few hundred years ago, when it was hunted to extinction by the colonizers of the time, the Maori. Any unsuspecting medieval voyager who stepped ashore and spotted one would be forgiven for thinking that they were looking at a cockatrice (or velociraptor).

We also know that ancient Chinese apothecaries used fossilized bones in their medicines because their descendants guided western fossil-hunters to the same fossil caves. But what would they make of a fossilized Tyrannosaurus Rex skull? How could they not assume dragons?

Our genetic ancestors were once hunted by dinosaurs. Could dragons resonate as a deep compound symbol for one of our oldest foes?

ABOVE: In the early 1840's Sir Richard Owen coined the word "dinosaur", meaning "fearfully great lizard." It is reasonable to wonder whether the fossilised remains of these creatures gave rise to the many tales of dragons. After all, fossils have been discovered the world over and perhaps this explains why dragons are represented in so many different cultural contexts.
LEFT: The giant Moa bird; and a sea horse, without a shadow of a doubt a baby dragon.

THE EARTH DRAGON
and her fire-breathing core

What has scales, breathes fire and flies? Not only dragons, but the Earth does too. Throughout this book we have seen the figure of the dragon associated with elusive currents and energies, from the Chinese art of Feng Shui to the enigmatic French Wouivre, whether looking for the dragon's backbone in a line of hills in the aboriginal bush or following a medieval dragon-line of ancient churches across Europe.

It was only in the last half of the twentieth century, years after mankind had split the atom, discovered dinosaurs and photographed distant galaxies, that scientists finally realized that the whole earth was very like a scaly fire-breathing dragon. A huge continuous backbone of mountains runs down the center of every ocean on Earth, spewing fire and new rock underwater to form the ocean floor, which spreads out on both sides, carrying the continental plates apart. Elsewhere, plates collide, and ocean floor is subducted back into the molten mantle beneath the ancient floating continents. The story of the Earth is locked into its stones, as pressure gradients, magnetic reversals, crystal and mineral seams and wind and water patterns. Perhaps this is the dragon the ancients were referring to. Perhaps we have been living on a dragon all along.

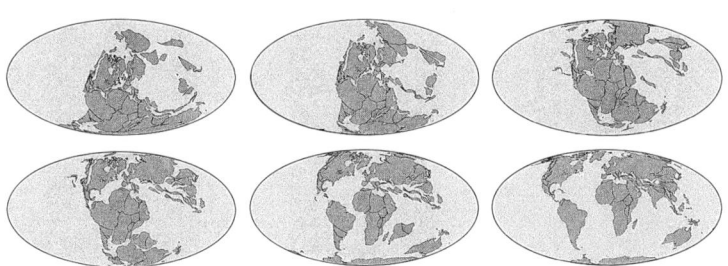

ABOVE: *The tectonic plates underlying the Americas, Europe and Eastern Asia (courtesy of the Smithsonian Institution). The Earth is a thinly covered ball of molten rock, the temperature at its centre being hotter than the surface of the sun.* FACING PAGE: *The plates shift and jostle, carrying the continents around. Fire-breathing volcanoes bring valuable minerals to the surface—the dragon guards her treasure.*

GAZETTEER OF INTERESTING DRAGON SITES

Aller, Somerset. The Flying Serpent. The giant winged serpent lived in a den on Round Hill until it was slain by the Lord of Aller with the help of several of his laborers. In Aller church there is an effigy of the knight while at nearby Low Ham Church is a spear said to be the one that killed the dragon

Anwick, Lincolnshire. The Drake. A field known as Drake Stone close was said to be the home of a treasure guarding dragon. A boulder in the field, now broken, is known as the 'Drake Stone'. 'Drake', an old name for a dragon was forgotten when the story was retold and the creature described, rising out of the ground, was a quacking duck

Bamburgh, Northumberland, England. The Laidly Worm of Spindlestone Heugh [see "Worm"]. The legend can be seen displayed at Bamburgh Castle; the Spindlestone, sometimes known as the Bridlestone, where the Worm coiled herself, can be seen nearby at Spindlestone Heugh.

Bisterne Park, Hampshire, England. The Fiery Dragon of Bistern. Sir Maurice de Berkeley slew a fire breathing dragon in an area called Dragon Field. His two dogs died in the battle, Sir Maurice died later. At Bisterne Park there is a carved dragon over the main entrance and statues of two dogs in the grounds.

Brent Pelham, Herts, England. The Brent Pelham Dragon. The Brent Pelham dragon dwelt in a cave under the roots of an old yew tree that stood on the boundary of Great and little Peppersall Fields. The local church contains the tomb of Piers Shonks who was reputed to have killed the savage Brent Pelham dragon by thrusting his spear down its throat at nearby Peppsall Field.

Brinsop, Hereford & Worcester, England. St. George Slays the Dragon. The church at Brinsop is dedicated to St George and has a fine tympanum showing the saint spearing a worm-like dragon. The dragon lived in Dragon's Well in Duck's Pool meadow to the south of the church and the bare patch in Lower Stanks field is said to be the place where the dying dragon's blood poisoned the earth. Close by is Wormsley village.

Bures, Essex, England. The Elusive dragon. A 13th century wall painting of a dragon in nearby Wissington may be the likeness of a dragon who was sighted here briefly in 1405.

Cnoc-na-Cnoimh, Dumfries and Galloway, Scotland. The Worm of Cnoc-na Cnoimh. A farmer, Hector Gunn, killed the Worm because he could not stand its poisonous breath. He used a spear on the tip of which was a lump of peat soaked in boiling pitch which he thrust down the worm's throat. The hillside, Cnoc-na-Cnoimh means wormhill, is ringed by spiral undulations said to have been caused by the worm in its death throes.

Crowcombe, Somerset, England. The Gurt Vurm of Shervage Wood. Crowcombe Church contains bench end carvings of men and dragons fighting and dragons with foliage issuing from their mouths. When the Vurm was cut in two by a woodsman, one end went to Bilbrook where a dragon can be seen on a wall painting in Cleeve Abbey, there is also a hotel in Bilbrook called 'The Dragon House' and Dragon Cross is nearby. The other half of the Vurm went to Kingston St. Mary where there is another dragon killing legend, perhaps it was the other half of the Vurm.

Dalry, dumfries and Galloway, Scotland The White Serpent The lord of Galloway offered a reward to whomsoever would kill a corpse eating giant serpent that lived in Dalray coiled around Mote Hill. A blacksmith gained the reward by covering himself with spikes and goading the serpent into swallowing him. The spikes tore the serpent to pieces and for three days the waters of the Ken ran red with blood.

Deerhurst, Gloucestershire, England. The Deerhurst Dragon. A laborer, John Smith won an estate on Walton Hill by killing a dragon. He fed it with milk until it relaxed and went to sleep, Then he took his axe and chopped off its head. The church has a number of stone heads said to be dragon's heads; over the outer doors, the inner doors, a window and the chancel arch.

Dinas Emrys, Snowdonia, Wales. The Red and White Fighting Dragons [see "Dragons in Heraldry"]. Remains of an Iron age hill fort can be seen on the top of Dinas Emrys. The area is private land.

Handale, Yorkshire, England. The Handale Worm. A gallant youth named Scaw slew the Handale Worm, rescued an earl's daughter and married her. In the now demolished Benedictine Handale Priory a stone coffin was found which contained an Elizabethan sword. It was said to be that of the dragon slayer. Scaw Wood, a wood bearing the name of the dragon killer is nearby.

Henham, Essex, England. The Essex Serpent. The serpent was first mentioned in a pamphlet in 1669. It was described as being about eight feet long with large eyes, fierce looking teeth and very small wings. It was sighted several times before it disappeared. There is a medieval carving of a dragon in St. Mary's Church at Henham.

Horsham, Sussex, England. The Dragon of St.Leonard's Forest. In St. Leonard's forest with it's great old trees and hammer ponds is Dragon Inn, beds of lilly-of-the-valley mark the place where St Leonard's blood is said to have flowed and changed into these flowers as he fought the dragon; lilly-of-the-valley is one of the symbols of the coming of Christ.

Kellington, West Yorkshire, England. The Serpent of Kellington. The surrounding woodlands harboured a giant serpent who devoured all the sheep in the area. A shepherd aided by his dog and wielding a crook eventually killed the monster although both shepherd and dog died in the attempt. Kellington Church contains the Kellington Serpent Stone, a monument carved with a cross, on one side is a weathered serpent and on the other a human figure and an animal.

Ker Moor, Somerset, England. St. Carantoc's Serpent. A kinder fate befell a terrible serpent that devastated the landscape around Ker Moor. St. Carantoc approached the serpent who meekly allowed the saint to put his stole around its neck. Carantoc brought the serpent to King Arthur's stronghold but would not let it be killed. He ordered it to go away and never return and this it did. King Arthur's stronghold is said to be Dunster Castle and Ker Moor was where the serpent dwelt.

Kilve, Somerset, England. Blue Ben. In the museum at Taunton is the skull of an ichthyosaurus which, at one time according to legend, was said to be that of a dragon called Blue Ben. The dragon lived on Putsham Hill and drowned in the mud at Kilve.

Kirkton of Strathmartin, Angus, Scotland. The Legend of Nine Tempting Maidens [see Worm]. Martin's Stone where Martin killed a dragon, after it had eaten nine maidens when they went to a well at Pitempton, can be seen in a field to the north of Baldragon Wood (below).

The dying dragon uttered these words:-
"I was tempit at Pitempton,
Draiglet [dragged] at Baldragon,
Striken at Strikemartin,
And killed at Martinstane."

These are all place names in the surrounding area. Nine Maiden's well has been filled in and can no longer be seen.

Lake Cynwch, Dolgellau, Gwynedd, Wales. The Wyvern of Cynwch Lake. The Wyvern lived in the lake until it was killed by a shepherd lad with the help of the inhabitants of the Monastery of the Standard. There is a National Trust footpath around the edge of the lake and Cymmer Abbey [The Monastery of the Standard] and a 20th century Druid stone circle are in the area.

Linton, Roxburghshire, Scotland. The Wyrm of Wyrmiston. This Wyrm was killed by Norman Somerville, Laird of Larriston who thrust a lance, tipped with a lump of peat dipped in scalding tar, down its throat. This is a similar technique to the slaying of the Cnoc-na-Cnoimh Worm. The contractions of the dying Wyrm coiled round Wormington Hill marked the hill with vermicular traces. Somerville was created Baron of

Linton and given the post of Royal Falconer. In Linton Church there is a carving of a man, with a creature that could be a falcon, slaying a dragon.

Llandeilo Graham, Powys, Wales. The Dragon in the Tower. The local church tower was the roosting place of a terror inspiring dragon. A cunning plough boy made a dummy of a dragon with knives and hooks sticking out of it and placed it in the tower when the dragon was away. The dragon returned, attacked the dummy and was impaled upon its spikes. It is thought that this legend was inspired by a draconian weather vane that used to be on the church tower.

Longwitton, Thurston, Northumberland, England The Wells of the Invisible Dragon. The people of Longwitton were unable to use their three wells because they sensed the presence of a dragon although it was invisible. The legendary hero Guy of Warwick was passing though by and agreed to fight the dragon as he had a magic eye ointment that enabled him to see his adversary (below).

After a prodigious fight, Guy was able to kill the dragon and the local people were able to use the healing wells again.

Lyminster, Sussex, England, The Knuckler. The Knuckler lived in an almost bottomless pool called The Knuckler Hole which can be seen north west of Lyminster near the church which contains a Norman coffin lid called the Slayer's Stone said to belong to the Knuckler's killer.

Middlewich, Cheshire, England. The Moston Dragon. Sir Thomas Venables shot a dragon in the eye at Bache Pool at Moston just as it was about to eat a small child. The family crest is a dragon with a child in its mouth. Perhaps the legend was a misinterpretation of a heraldic drawing [see Heraldry]. Middlewich Church has a chapel dedicated to the Venables family.

Mordiford, Hereford & Worcester, England. The Mordiford Dragon. The dragon was killed, by a villain called Garston, as it slithered down Serpent Lane to the River Lugg. Garston hid in an iron spiked barrel and persuaded the dragon to attack him; it was cut to pieces on the spikes. There was once a painting of the dragon on the wall of the church but it was destroyed in 1810.

Nunnington, Yorkshire. England, The Dragon of Loschy Hill. Peter Loschy slew a dragon on a hill by wearing a suit of armour studded with sharp blades which cut the dragon to pieces when it tried to crush him. Both Peter and his dog died when they touched the dragon's poisonous blood. The place of the battle is now named Loschy Hill. Nearby Nunnington Church contains a tomb of a knight with his feet partly destroyed resting on what could be the remains of a dog or a lion. However the tomb has no identification and is considered too old to apply here.

Penshaw, Durham, England, The Lambton Worm. Worm Hill around which the Worm coiled can be seen in North Biddick on the bank of the Wear River. Also to be seen is a replica of the well where the worm spent its formative years; and according to legend 'growed and growed, and growed to an awful size.'

Renwick, Cumberland, England. The Renwick Cockatrice. This strange creature escaped from the foundations of the local church when it was demolished. John Tallantine killed the dragon using the branch of the rowan tree which is reputed to have magical powers.

Slingsby, Yorkshire, England. The Long Slingsby Serpent. A local hero, Wyvill, and his dog slew the dragon which was documented as being either one mile or eighteen yards long but both perished in the attempt. The coat of arms of the Wyvilles has a Wyvern upon it. The serpent dwelt in a large hole, probably a disused limestone quarry which looked like a cup-like hollow, half a mile from the town.

Sockburn, County Durham, England. The Sockburn Worm. The legend of the variously named Sockburn Worm, dragon, wyvern or ask is one of the oldest in the country. Sir John Conyers killed the Worm with a weapon called the Conyer's Falchion which is still used in the inauguration rites of the bishops of Durham. The falchion can be seen in Durham Cathedral Treasury. In the grounds of Sockburn Hall is the remains of a church containing an effigy of a knight in armour with a lion fighting a dragon at its feet. A manuscript in the British Museum recounts the legend.

Uffington, Oxfordshire, England, SU3089 Another Site of St. George Killing the Dragon. Below the chalk-hill figure of the White Horse of Uffington in the White Horse Vale is Dragon Hill where, again, there is a bald patch of ground where the dragon's dying blood is said to have poisoned the earth. In Saxon times King Certic's warriors were said to have slain the Pendragon Naud and his army here, perhaps that is how it got its name. It has been suggested that the stylised chalk carving here is a dragon and not a horse.

Wantley, Yorkshire. England. The Dragon of Wantley. A 17th century ballad recounts the story of the fate of the dragon of Wantley. The dragon is described as having forty four teeth of iron, long claws, a sting in his tail, a tough hide and two wings, It lived in Yorkshire near Rotherham and the people thereabouts begged More of More Hall to kill it. He agreed in exchange for a fair maid of sixteen and armed with the traditional spiked armour he fought the beast for two days and two nights. Eventually More kicked the dragon in a vulnerable place, his arsehole, which ended the creature's life. The scene of the ballad is a place called Warncliffe Lodge, generally known as Wantley, a mile from the village called Wortley. The More coat of arms bears a green dragon.

Wherwell, Hampshire, England, SU9676. The Wherwell Cockatrice. This monster, hatched by a toad incubating a duck's egg, lived in a crypt beneath Werwell Priory and caused much devastation in the surrounding area. A man called Green destroyed the cockatrice by lowering a polished metal mirror into its den. The cockatrice fiercely attacked its own reflection in the mirror with such vigour that it killed itself. There is an area called Green's acre at Wherwell. There was said to be a weather vane in the shape of a cockatrice on a tower there but no trace of it now exists.

Wiston, Pembrokeshire, Wales. The Wiston Cockatrice. Centuries ago, there were several claimants to the estate of Castle Gwys, now known as Wiston. It was agreed by the family that if anyone of them could observe a multi-eyed cockatrice, who lived in a hole in a bank near the castle, without it seeing him would gain the estate. One wily claimant devised a plan; he secured himself in a barrel and peered at the cockatrice through its bunghole as the barrel rolled down the hill past the cockatrice's lair. This stratagem won him the estate.

APPENDIX - CHINESE DRAGONS

NINE CLASSICAL DRAGON TYPES:
(Chinese dragons are thought of as male, or 'yang', and are generally benevolent, holy and auspicious).

Tianlong, The Celestial Dragon
Shenlong, the Spiritual Dragon
Fucanglong, the Dragon of Hidden Treasures
Dilong, the Underground Dragon
Yinglong, the Winged Dragon
Jiaolong, the Horned Dragon
Panlong, the Coiling Dragon: lives in water
Huanglong, Yellow Dragon, emerged from the River Luo to show Fuxi how to write
Dragon King, one for each of the four directions

DRAGON CHILDREN:
(normally nine, but more are known, found in architectural and monumental decorations)

Baxia, sometimes Bixi, (Genbu in Japan), the first son, looks like a giant tortoise. He represents the element of rock and earth, is very strong and is often found as the carved stone base of monumental tablets.

Chiwen (the phoenix Suzaku in Japan), the second son, is a dragon who can see a long way and generally decorates the corners of rooftops. Sometimes called **Chaofeng**, while Chiwen becomes the Ridge-Swallowing beast, who rules rainfall and safeguards buildings from fire.

Pulao (Seiryuu in Japan), the third son, resembles a small blue dragon. He represents the elements of water and wind, likes to roar and is always found on musical instruments and bells.

Bi'an (Byakko in Japan), the fourth son, looks like a white tiger. Incredibly powerful, he tells good from bad and is found at court and on prison doors. He represents the metal element.

Taotie, the fifth son, loves eating and is found on food-related wares. He is often swapped for **Qiuniu**, a dragon who is fond of music and decorates the bridge of stringed instruments, or Fuxi, who loves literature and is carved on the sides of inscribed stone tablets.

Gongfu, the sixth son, likes to be in water. His dragon's head is found on bridges.

Yazi, the seventh son, loves fighting and is found on sword and knife hilts and battle axes.

Suanmi, the eighth son, looks like a lion and is fond of smoke and fire. He is guards the main door and is often found on incense burners.

Jiaotu, the youngest son, looks like a conch or clam and is tight-lipped, and does not like to be disturbed. He appears on the front door, the door knocker or the doorstep.

There are also two inferior, malevolent (rare for Chinese dragons) and hornless dragon species, the jiao and the li. The jiao are female dragons and the li are yellow jiao.

Bench End from Crowcombe Church, UK.

58